STRANGER

LAURA SIMS

Cover art   "Betty" by Gerhard Richter
Oil on canvas, 1988
40 1/4 x 28 1/2 in. (102.2 x 72.4 cm)
Courtesy of the Saint Louis Art Museum

Book layout by   Colie Collen
Book design by   Fence Books

Published in the United States by   Fence Books
Science Library 320
University at Albany
1400 Washington Avenue
Albany, NY 12222
www.fenceportal.org

Fence Books are distributed by   University Press of New England
www.upne.com

and printed in Canada by   Westcan Printing Group
www.westcanpg.com

Library of Congress Cataloguing in Publication Data
        Sims, Laura [1973–]
        Stranger/ Laura Sims

Library of Congress Control Number: 2009924811

ISBN 1-934200-23-9
ISBN 13: 978-1-934200-23-0

FIRST EDITION

FENCE BOOKS are published in partnership with the University at Albany and the New York State Writers Institute, and with help from the New York State Council on the Arts, the National Endowment for the Arts, and the friends of *Fence*.

STRANGER

LAURA SIMS

ALBANY, NEW YORK

ACKNOWLEDGMENTS

This book is also dedicated to the memory of my grandmother, Jane Roessler.

I would not have been able to complete this book without the generous allotment of time and financial support provided by the Japan–US Friendship Commission's Creative Artists Exchange Fellowship.

I would like to thank the following publications for having published poems, sometimes in earlier versions, from this collection: *Crayon, Fascicle, Milk, Octopus, Onedit, Parcel, Rooms Outlast Us, Square One, Tarpaulin Sky,* and *Tryst.* Special thanks to Roberto Harrison, editor of Bronze Skull Press, who published earlier versions of poems from the section "Blank" in a chapbook called *Corrections.*

I thank my stepfather, Joe Teefey, who shared much of this particular journey, and cared for and protected me along the way.

For their constant friendship, love, and support in all kinds of weather, I thank: Courtney Brkic, Stephanie Fiorelli and Adam Koehler, Pam Gray, Anthony Hawley, Melanie Hoftyzer, Lynn Keller, Margaret Lewis, David Markson, Chris and Karen Mead, Ken, Inge-Grete and Caitlin Mead, Hermine Meinhard, Kazuko Minamoto, Rongal Nikora, Danielle Pafunda, David and Amy Pavelich, Danielle Pollack, Elizabeth Robinson, Gomi Sims-Mead, Robert and Marcia Sims, Maya Smukler, Stacy Szymaszek and Erica Kaufman, and Judy Teefey.

I thank my Baruch students, who make teaching so joyful and rewarding that it doesn't seem right to call it a "job" anymore.

For his love, encouragement, and indispensable feedback, I thank my husband, Corey Mead.

Finally, a huge thank you to Rebecca Wolff for providing such wise editorial guidance along the way.

For my mother, Anne Teefey
(1943–1992)

BLANK (1943–1973)

Seemed to have crossed a dark lake

Or ring

Or starry circle of some kind

Across which

Numbers

Actually mean

To be part of the dreadful thing

She began the world

(Now close the reverberating door

1

She points to the side, and the camera swings—

Behind her: a trim midriff and shapely legs

She smiles and gestures, nodding her head, beckoning as she backs up,
backs into her mother, and curls away from us, smiling into her mother's
skirt, moving her lips against the soft, scratchy fabric.

She makes sounds

But no sound

Survives

Except silk

"Came back with a vengeance

After the war"

In her holiday dress for the world

Whitewashed for her

[Her father filming the primitive living room dance]

With gravity

Worn like a bonnet of lead

Above her the world, the plain, and the barrow

[Still for a moment]

In pictures come softly, blurry and sweet

at the edges. She gets so close to the lens that her face

dissolves. What's left is a red-and-white blur by the tinseled pine.

And her mother's grin.

And her father directing her: backwards, forwards, a bit to the side. She grows

Up.

How am I?

Now?

The way she loves her

Hair down her back

The onlookers'

Darling...

Her mouth opens

Teeth?
Underground

Pool?
Underground

Estate?
Underground: Moments before, in the sudden light.

"All this," she says, spreading her arms to the ocean.

"All this," her friend echoes, leaning over the rail.

The sharp wind reddens their faces, tangles their hair. They laugh open-mouthed. She can't say where she comes from now—Ocean? Sky?

The water keeps hanging us up

Are we bored

And in heaven

Or France—

The old gentleman wagging

His finger over

His head, to the right

Mouth full of bread

And leaning

Against an anonymous car

Baguette in one hand, acres

Of country surround

[My mother]

Had never

Been so undone

Old-World Romance Ends

Are you cold

they ask, did he touch you, they ask

Did you suffer

She made it through

Joy, humming

The song cut in half

To the Midwest sky

*

The haunting last phrase of it

Brings to mind

Yellows
(Sunlit)—

Her myriad past

She stretches out on the lawn with her parents above her, *crisp* and approving.

Home at last.

*

Later she lies on the rug in the china-blue living room.

*

The bottles & vases / of hand-blown glass / in the window / filter / a sickly light.

In pristine trappings she warms to the earth

Serene

In her taffeta dress

*

Her flesh basket

Calling whose howling

Is distant

But permanent

Pleasure

They walk through a shower of rice.

She stands at a window, recalling her mother's words: "ten years, twenty, two thousand and twenty, some beast. . . ."

Blood climbs to her face; she rattles the ice in her glass.

In their tiny house

The snow the snow the snow outside. She asks *what life*

Is this what life

With palms on her rounded stomach

Not yours, but another's

Sound—

Rang out

In the standard ways

[Is this what life

And then I existed

The universe

Yoked

To the stairs

At the back of my head]

ANOTHER COUNTRY (1992)

We were less involved with the lake

We asked for your name—in cups—along the way

You weren't thinking of us

You were thinking I look much better when thin

Willowy

These are the words we used to describe

Popsicle sticks on the dresser

A cup filled with bile

The sun slanting into that summer, a hammer

She lay dreaming under the knife while we

In our alien living room

A green wall reminds her of summer

Once pinned

Her hands

And then

Nothing

——The world grows thin——

Not fire nor water

Nor mere inundation

Nor ease

She sings between sleep

Her world is a stalker / she stalks it in turn and

The family mouth

Runs on

Those not worthy are scattered wide

The line

Coined lately

Gone

✳

My head—

And everyone

Changed

✳

And the Ancient of Days

Sweeping into me—

Describe

This impossible field, this wave

The morphine box

And flavored ice

*

Everything went on as usual, outside

I craved a great earthquake

Behind her eyes:

The stranger

His white corsage

In the corner

Relieved

By his teeth in the sun,

His mellifluous chatter

Something

Like respite

Confetti descends

But dampened leaves, danger—

A red and blue cloud—

Nothing

To stay these goings down of the sun

She felt

Those hidden things

From the pervious
Margin

*

I looked for myself
In myself

And the woods were vocal

Oh my
Divided mind

Made

*

In the grudgingly unified
Tower

A face

The face

I made

For you

The house stands still

No footprints, no blood on the carpet or walls

[Skew-eyed]

        *

The men come knocking at dawn yet nothing

Is overturned

        *

The hospital holds all the ugliness.

        *

My mother looks down at the page, dissatisfied.

        Dearest, it is with a sigh of relief that I write . . .

What breaks

Is small in the human eye

An inveterate inner dam

Leaves me washed

And willing

From the public mind

Into wilderness

When I move

The 'booms' and panics

Subside

This hour, no longer

My 'no' exists

On a manicured lawn of such green, the end

Of her middle-class life

In America

The world is stuffed, suspended in gelid blue.

*

When the elevator opens, we blink in sudden light.

Down the hall and beyond

*

It stuns me

It stuns me to be alive

It stuns me to be alive in the waffle house.

*

The sun looks bad.

I have no desire

For all we know

In a lukewarm bath

——Noise——

And another country

Heard from   ,

LETTERS FROM ELSEWHERE
PART I (1992)

Dear,

The lock broke

Your wishes
Are endless

You wrote
As are

Records of
consequence

We are endless

Imploring you

Please

In the library:
Something
Of note

Belongs in a box.

(It is still early days)

How we long
For your finest
Possession and how

It becomes you

Is it
Under a robe
A chair
A mahogany dresser

Is it
Flattened
Or rolled
And secured with a ribbon

A faded blue ribbon

Not even a

[blank]

Would elect

To be

*

Your wishes

Are

Ours

Are

Recalcitrant, fierce

Even we
Know our minds
When it comes

*

It is rightfully ours
Although yours

It was born
In our lands

Sick and wanting

But pure

And of creamiest hue

And as smooth

As your face

On that day

In its finish

There is no such thing as a copy

We know
Every line
Every whorl
Every watermark

Stain spot & incident

Lending itself to design

Not yours, but

Mine

✱

They say

Legacy burns

When reversed

Or undone
Or corrected
Smoothed over
Or
Smoothed in a mound

We are waiting

Dear girl

Come rattle the chains when you
Come

By the throat

*

Do not fail

But

Deliver it

LETTERS FROM ELSEWHERE
PART 2 (1993)

We fear
By the library door

Any news?

We fear you might fail

May it waft in and hang
In the air of our room

One night

We've been twiddling our thumbs
Braiding our hair

By the fire

Telling tales

We fear you might fail

That final directive

Clean and un-creased
As clean and as creamy

As when

It was born

'A man is always
doing something'

We've heard

Being dead means
No more listening to the radio

Go along

Unknowing if the elk was real

Patted down hard
Smoothed in an oval
Planted with grass

When you stumbled out raw

A white satin-lined carriage

Look harder

You sleeping too much

What it means is
Crossing the bridge into fog

As clean and un-creased
Make it pure

Or some other such nonsense

We love the girl

Who turns

To us:

Make it clean as your face

On that day

Golden chain

Run come rattle the chain

Darling

At our gates

Sick and wanting

Have you any idea
We've expected

Not this

Half-laughing / half-weeping

'Not for us'

This particular consequence

Any news

Un-clean and un-creamy

Un-Darling

Alive with its absence

You, stained

ELSEWHERE (1992–   )

A final capsule:

The world

In the zero

Held

For a moment

*

Her yellow, curled hands

Simply walked from the room

(No

Carrying on

They rouse themselves, and are not themselves

*

One of them rests

In herself

*

(She is never herself.

Red rings circle her eyes.)

She rises up

Slowly

Who she has been . . .

*

Obscene,

Is what she

Herself

What is

Otherwise atrium light,

Greco-Romans

Horribly

Soft and alive

She is water poured out

Through irrational doorways

∗

The Somewhat forms

An unreal skin

And a sovereign clearness

Designs

Her feet

In the modeless "where"

∗

Now the world is

No more than an alien terror, or

No more an alien terror

From her mud plateau

She insists on a universe

Two stories deep

A bell with a crack

Is a mushroom born between night

And the rest

*

Her unreal hands

At the banquet

*

I have been swallowed up

In a grove—

Say nothing

Become

What matter becomes

In the rushing together / charade for the abstract heaven

Of worlds

*

The sun warms me—

Isn't it strange?

*

She is twofold

A compound

There is no going out of one's heart

To belief

*

You return, replete

That shape am I, that scent

The wildcat takes human shape

On the rock—

No end

Wherever we went the mountains followed

You shuffled behind

In your long pearl dress, ridiculous

Lily

Pinned to your chest

Come on

The mountains are gaining

Have eyes

For those flimsy white curtains

My hand, too small for gathering

The animals, ashamed

And entered the Road of the Sun

*

A dried leaf—

I was afraid

The valley was deaf

And cluttered with occupants

*

The world was old with spoiled arts.

The dry dust billowed in the marketplace.

*

I almost

Passed into a land

Amidst the new debris

A god & man, an animal & man, a corner

Of her scarlet robe

They had no time to call it names

Thanksgiving: the barn-like restaurant

We scraped

And numbed, blind

*

Long after the fact

*

The lowness

Of pilgrimage managed

Through deep sand to the store

We burned

Powder

Shot

Sugar

Trees

More

And beyond them were more

Mother, the keys are

You know where

*

Each part sings against

Knowing your part

Of the rock-face:

Kingdom of air

*

You know how they are

Those words

*

How they unman the animals

The floating signs along the road

Home

Say

Mother are you   Mother are you   Mother are you

Mother are you   Mother are you   Mother are you

Driving it

"Bound together, we matter"

[She touches

The places she touched]

Red brick, patent shoes

A white linen dress

What floated off earth

Like so many

Handfuls of fluff

＊

If tied, we assume

What the footage assumes:

Dissent cannot undo

An end or

An origin

Fence Books

THE MOTHERWELL PRIZE

Aim Straight at the Fountain and Press Vaporize Elizabeth Marie Young
Unspoiled Air Kaisa Ullsvik Miller

THE ALBERTA PRIZE

The Cow Ariana Reines
Practice, Restraint Laura Sims
A Magic Book Sasha Steensen
Sky Girl Rosemary Griggs
The Real Moon of Poetry and Other Poems Tina Brown Celona
Zirconia Chelsey Minnis

FENCE MODERN POETS SERIES

Star in the Eye James Shea
Structure of the Embryonic Rat Brain Christopher Janke
The Stupefying Flashbulbs Daniel Brenner
Povel Geraldine Kim
The Opening Question Prageeta Sharma
Apprehend Elizabeth Robinson
The Red Bird Joyelle McSweeney

NATIONAL POETRY SERIES

Collapsible Poetics Theater Rodrigo Toscano

ANTHOLOGIES & CRITICAL WORKS

*Not for Mothers Only: Contemporary Poets on Child-Getting &
Child-Rearing*   Catherine Wagner & Rebecca Wolff, editors

A Best of Fence: *The First Nine Years, Volumes 1 & 2*   Rebecca Wolff &
Fence Editors, editors

POETRY

Stranger	Laura Sims
The Method	Sasha Steensen
The Orphan & Its Relations	Elizabeth Robinson
Site Acquisition	Brian Young
Rogue Hemlocks	Carl Martin
19 Names for Our Band	Jibade Khalil Huffman
Infamous Landscapes	Prageeta Sharma
Bad Bad	Chelsey Minnis
Snip Snip!	Tina Brown Celona
Yes, Master	Michael Earl Craig
Swallows	Martin Corless-Smith
Folding Ruler Star	Aaron Kunin
The Commandrine & Other Poems	Joyelle McSweeney
Macular Hole	Catherine Wagner
Nota	Martin Corless-Smith
Father of Noise	Anthony McCann
Can You Relax in My House	Michael Earl Craig
Miss America	Catherine Wagner

FICTION

Flet: A Novel	Joyelle McSweeney
The Mandarin	Aaron Kunin